IMAGES OF ENGLAND

PORTCHESTER

This group enjoying themselves at the Waterside represents many of the families living in Portchester at the time. The event may have been a sailing club regatta, in which most of the village used to take part, or just a warm day in the summer. The north wall of the Roman fort is in the background here, in around 1927. Adults, from left to right, are Mrs Knocker, Mrs Adams, Mrs Wilson (née Adams), Mrs Timbury (née Catmore), Frank Catmore and his sister, Jenny, in the chair. Children, from left to right, are Kathleen Towse (later Wells), Barbara Wilson (later Watson), Jean Knocker (later Duce), Ray Timbury, Phyllis Timbury (later Spence) and Vera Towse (later Partridge).

IMAGES OF ENGLAND

PORTCHESTER

DEREK E. PEARCE, BRIAN A. TAYLOR
AND E. JOHN TOWSE

This book is dedicated to The Portchester Society in their Silver Jubilee year. The Portchester Society, formed in 1978, to 'Promote, Protect and Preserve' Portchester, has worked hard over the last twenty-five years to achieve these objectives. We gratefully acknowledge all those members past and present who have contributed to the aims of the society.

First published in 2003 by Tempus Publishing Limited

Reprinted in 2010 by
The History Press
The Mill, Brimscombe Port,
Stroud, Gloucestershire, GL5 2QG
www.thehistorypress.co.uk

©Derek E. Pearce, Brian A. Taylor, E. John Towse 2010

The right of Derek E. Pearce, Brian A. Taylor and
E. John Towse to be identified as the Authors
of this work has been asserted in accordance with the
Copyrights, Designs and Patents Act 1988.

All rights reserved. No part of this book may be reprinted
or reproduced or utilised in any form or by any electronic,
mechanical or other means, now known or hereafter invented,
including photocopying and recording, or in any information
storage or retrieval system, without the permission in writing
from the Publishers.

British Library Cataloguing in Publication Data.
A catalogue record for this book is available from the British Library.

ISBN 978 0 7524 2845 1

Typesetting and origination by Tempus Publishing Limited
Printed and bound in England

Contents

Acknowledgements		6
Introduction		7
1.	The Castle and Environment	9
2.	Churches and Chapels	19
3.	Schools and Education	29
4.	Residents and Personalities	39
5.	The Village, Roads and Streets	49
6.	Pageants, Galas and Outings	79
7.	Listed Buildings and Old Houses	89
8.	Trades and Transport	99
9.	Surrounding Features	115
10.	Sport, Sailing and Leisure	119

The stone sign on the roundabout, designed by Felicity Patrick, seventeen, a pupil of Portchester Community School. This site was always referred to as 'The Cross Roads' and still is by many long-term residents. This is the position where north-south Castle Street meets Station Road and is crossed by the east-west main road (A27), in 2002. The photograph was taken in 2002.

Acknowledgements

Many people have contributed to this book, in a variety of ways. We cannot name them all, only express our sincere gratitude for all their input. However two exceptional contributions must be mentioned. Des Biggs hired an aircraft and took many aerial views to compare with the earlier record, as well as contributing to a contemporary record for the future. Mike Goodall gave us complete access to his considerable collection of original postcards and Portchester artefacts, collected over a period of more than thirty years. The Portchester Society archive has been made freely available.

We should like to thank the Curator and Staff of Westbury Museum, Fareham for their help. Our appreciation is also extended to Mrs Rosemary Dunne and Mrs Jacky Taylor for checking the draft documents.

Some of the other photographs are copies or originals from the lifetime work and collection of the late Geo T. Crouch and these we acknowledge with admiration for his artistry. The Portsmouth newspapers have contributed a number of Portchester images over many years and we thank them for their photographs or unrealized copies.

Attempts to determine the origins of many photographs have met with little success and we apologise if we have inadvertently caused any distress by our inability to trace the photographers.

Introduction

The birth of the settlement at Portchester is lost in the mists of pre-Roman times. Fact and legend merge until the time of the building of the Roman fortress. The first name of the ancient British site on the small peninsula seems to have been 'Caer Peris', attributed to one of two quarrelling brothers, both killed, perhaps over possession of the site. Some of the physical legacy left by the Romans, Normans, Saxons and later occupiers is clear to see, well preserved in and around the magnificent Roman fort. Early physical evidence of the native inhabitants is much harder to find. Kings and Queens of England have progressed up and down the ancient and delightful Castle Street, once called South Street, from early times up until the reign of Elizabeth I. King John was one of the most frequent visitors.

There is now a wealth of written history on Portchester ranging from the romantic to the detailed academic. The first 'modern' documented evidence of the name appears in the Domesday Book. There, on one page, the extended spelling dispute regarding the first 't' is well illustrated – in one paragraph the 't' is in place, while the next paragraph leaves it out! Officially the 't' was permanently added only 150 years ago, by the then Jurors of Portchester Castle, who decided that 'Port' was preferable to 'Por', as 'Port-town' was felt to be more appropriate than 'Poor-town'.

From the eighteenth century onwards, drawings, sketches and eventually photographs begin to appear in ever-greater numbers. We have sought to avoid, where possible, reproducing illustrations that have been used in previous publications. Some local readers may be disappointed that their favourites are not included. We can only say that some appear in the suggested further reading.

Also, many residents have good long memories and they will recognize themselves or relatives in the early photographs. Unfortunately, space restricts printing all the names under the various groups of people, even if all of them were known. However, we should certainly be pleased to add additional evidence to the increasing archive of information held by The Portchester Society.

Portchester has grown since the beginning of the twentieth century. From a population of about 900 in 1900 it now verges on 19,000. Not for the first time has the village seen such a great increase, as during the Napoleonic Wars the combination of villagers and prisoners – both French and otherwise – saw the population swell to some 10,000. Medieval populations also varied enormously.

Things have changed in Portchester today, and the farming and market gardening of the early 1900s has been replaced, largely, by streets and housing with some light industry. Fortunately the area surrounding the old settlement has become increasingly protected by preservation orders and hopefully will remain so for future generations.

Apart from the castle, the meadows to the north east of Castle Street also show Waring's factory as it was in 1948, before the site was cleared for landscaping and light industrial development up to the main A27 road. The cricket pavilion can be seen on what was then Waring's sports field, just to the left of 'Boat Island' by the banks. A number of occupied houseboats were permanently moored along the banks down to the 'Waterside', by the castle.

Suggested Further Reading

Anon, *Portchester Castle – Its Origin, History and Antiquities*. Interspersed with anecdotes of its occupation during the late French Wars. Published at Portsea by W. Woodward, Common Hard (1849).

Lt Col J.H. Cooke, *Portchester Castle – Its Romance in Tradition and History*, privately published (1928). Now reprinted, 2008. Published by Albion Books, Portchester. ISBN 978-0-9560485-0-9

Professor Barry Cunliffe, Southampton University, '*Studies in Local History: Portchester*', The Portsmouth Papers, No. 1. Published by City Council, Portsmouth Corporation (1967).

C.E. Cooper, *Prisoners at Portchester*, Portsmouth Museum Society (1973).

Various guide books to the castle and church, written by St Mary's church vicars over the years. Including:

Revd J.D. Henderson, M.A. *Guide and History of Portchester Castle*.

Revd Canon Vaughan, *A Short Illustrated History of Portchester Castle*, W.H. Barrell, Portsmouth (c. 1900).

Professor Barry Cunliffe et al, *Excavations at Portchester Castle*, 5 Volumes (1975-1985).

Alan Montgomery, *My Goodness! My Portchester*, (1984).

George T. Crouch, *The Story of Portchester*, (1982).

Edgar Long, 'Portchester Memories after the First World War', *Hampshire Magazine*, Vol. 33, No. 10 (1993).

Eric James Barber, *The story of Portchester Castle*, The Front Page Press (1982).

J.T. Mumby, *Portchester Castle*, Official guide by English Heritage (1990).

Barbara Curtiss, *Fresh Air. A Childhood in Portchester*, (2003). ISBN 0-9537697-1-2

E.J. Towse, *Portchester Historic Plaques*. Published by The Portchester Society, (2006).

Portchester in Living Memory edited by Bryan Jerrard and Paul Woodman. Published by The Portchester Civic Society, (2006).

Dr Peter Barr-Taylor and E. John Towse, *Portchester Lake and The Sailing Club*, (2007).

Fiction:

Sir Walter Besant, *Holy Rose*, Chatto & Windus (1891).

Walter Besant and James Rice, *By Celia's Arbour*, (1878).

Keith H Vignoles, *A Prisoner of Portchester*, Published by Ian Harrap at The Peltham: Havant (1977).

One
The Castle and Environment

Portchester Castle, a Grade 1 listed building, seen from Portchester Lake in the early morning. This photograph was taken by Bob Turp from his boat in 1992.

The castle before the sea promenade was constructed to protect the walls. Parts of the earlier coastline, which has greatly changed over the years, may be detected in this 1920s view.

The construction of the inner bailey was essentially medieval, incorporating the original Roman walls. In the early twentieth century the keep and walls were left to nature until the Ministry of Works started extensive restoration in around 1900.

The approach to the land gate of the outer bailey, showing the outer walls prior to restoration. One of the girls with the pushchair is likely to be Nellie Bradley (later Mundy), with her brother in the chair. This was around 1907.

The custodian's wooden bungalow, here pictured in around 1930, much changed since it was erected around 1800 as a Napoleonic guardhouse. It has also served as a Sunday school, a dairy and a refreshment shop until, following the custodian's occupation, it was demolished in 1962 to provide a clear view of the impressive land gate.

The medieval entrance to the inner bailey and keep, c. 1910. The outer bailey was used for grazing livestock and the fence was necessary for their enclosure.

The tree-lined path leading to the church lych-gate and the castle water gate, c. 1928. Most of the trees were horse chestnuts. They remained until well into the 1950s.

Castle Street, formerly South Street, was almost the only occupied area of Portchester in the early part of the twentieth century, with a population of about 900. Many of the fields and meadows were still used for agriculture. This view dates from around 1905.

An equivalent aspect from the top of the keep, showing the expansion of the original village.

The water gate in the centre of the east wall, c. 1910. Possibly it replaced a much wider Roman gate. On high tides the sea lapped the ancient walls until 1936 when the present sea wall was constructed.

Looking though the water gate to the sea in Portchester Lake, c. 1910. The old hard leading down to the low water mark can still be seen. The dark blocks in the arch are of ironstone.

A late eighteenth-century engraving of the two-storey barrack blocks outside the north wall of the castle, c. 1784. They were used during the Napoleonic Wars for the militia guarding the predominately French prisoners.

The Powder House dates from the eighteenth century. Because of its explosive contents it was situated on the north outer defence bank, well away from the castle wall.

The Roman moat, pictured here in 1954, follows the three walls of the castle approachable by land. The sea completes the circumnavigation of the castle. Here, at the end of the moat, the sea is controlled for filling and flushing. On top of the old tunnel, under the sea wall, is the wooden windlass used to operate the gate. Over the past three or more generations the outflow to the sea has been known as 'The Trollop'.

The well-preserved Roman walls on the south side of the castle, viewed from the 'Urchins' meadows, c. 1920. In the background the original wooden masts of the Royal Naval radio station on Horsea Island are clearly visible.

The castle's outer earthworks defences date from the early fourteenth century. This section, shown here in around 1960, is on the west side. There are suggestions that the earth mounds could possibly be the defined borders of the pre-Roman settlement.

Outer defences continue round to the east, meeting the bank at Portchester Lake. They have long been a popular play area for local children and visitors.

Portchester peninsula and the castle from Portsdown Hill in around 1920, prior to the large expansion of population and light industry.

Near equivalent of the above view showing the expansion, c. 1965. The steam on the right is coming from Smith's crisp factory, now demolished. Vosper Thorneycroft's development into Portchester Lake is clearly defined.

Two

Churches and Chapels

The ancient priory church of St Mary, in the south-east corner of the castle, built for the Augustinian priory and founded here in around 1128. The priors had moved to Southwick by 1150, as the activity in and around the castle was said to be too noisy for monastic life. The cloister buildings have been demolished but the structure of the church remains little altered. St Mary's has served as the parish church for many centuries. This view dates from around 1905.

Lych-gate and early boundary wall, c. 1910. The original plaque reads,

> This lych-gate built in the year of her Majesty Queen Victoria's Diamond Jubilee 1897 was renovated and restored and this tablet erected by the people of Portchester as a memorial of the Silver Jubilee of His Majesty King George V 1935.

A second plaque commemorates the extensive renovation by volunteers in 1993.

The west front and entrance to St Mary's with its elaborately decorated entrance, 1950s. On the left, just above the column, can be seen a Pisces (fish) sign, which the Normans are said to have placed on all churches near the coast.

The interior of St Mary's church, prior to the arrival of electricity, c. 1920s. Oil lamps on the walls and choir stalls provided the only artificial light until 1933. Above the altar on the east wall is the stained-glass window, magnificent in early morning sunshine.

This font dates from around 1150 and is a fine example of carved Caen stone. It is considered to be one of the oldest Norman fonts in England. The sculpturing possibly represents Adam and Eve in the Garden of Eden or the Baptism of Christ. In 1888 the base was re-made replacing the one made in brick and plaster. This picture dates from around 1930.

This church organ, in the north transept, was hand-pumped for many years. If no parish volunteer was available, two choirboys were pressed into service. Note the oil lamps, still in use here in 1905, over the choir stalls.

This mystifying photograph was taken by Hazel Ray, a local resident, on a small instamatic camera in 1983. The event was a Portchester Gala and Flower Festival in the church. Sir Alec Rose, second in the line, opened the event. Neither the photographer nor her husband knew the church had been a priory in 1133. No one there at the time the picture was taken saw any object in the flower arrangement, and initially it was thought the photograph was spoilt.

The tomb of the Wyllie family. William Lionel Wyllie, the renowned Portsmouth marine artist, who died in 1931. After the service at Portsmouth Cathedral his body was carried up the harbour in a ten-oared cutter. At the castle water gate his body was transferred to a trek cart and conveyed to his last resting-place by a team of the 23rd Rover Sea Scouts.

William L. Wyllie, centre, with beard and monocle, with A.E. Stubbs, who was King's coxswain on the Royal yacht *Victoria & Albert*, behind him and Mr O'Hare, Roman Catholic headmaster, to his left. The senior Scout on his right represents Wyllie's long-term support of the Scouting movement. This rare picture dates from around 1921.

A sadly vandalized tombstone belonging to the Farmer family. This was the last resting-place of Emily Farmer, a very talented artist who lived with her mother and sister in Portchester House, Hospital Lane. Emily's most famous work was 'Kitty's Breakfast', dated 1883, now in the Victoria & Albert Museum. She often had local children sit for her. She died in 1905, aged seventy-eight.

This is one of the few remaining decorative tombstones in St Mary's churchyard. The inscription reads: 'Erected in loving memory of Janie Latham, aged 28, September 1885 [...] wife of Charles Latham, Captain Royal London Militia.' Mrs Jane Latham died on the yacht *St Bernard* in Portsmouth Harbour.

This is the Wesleyan Methodist church at the top of Castle Street. It was opened in 1933 and replaced the old chapel opposite Cow Lane, which became stables and is now a private dwelling. An even earlier Methodist church was situated at 131 Castle Street.

Church of Our Lady of Walsingham, the Roman Catholic church in White Hart Lane. It was opened in 1954, providing a local church for the increasing numbers of Catholic residents.

Procession of St Mary's church choir approaching the new mission church, near the west end of White Hart Lane, for the opening ceremony in May 1936. The lane is narrow and undeveloped with new houses just beginning to be built. Carrying the cross is Norman Daventry, who sadly lost his life in the Second World War.

The Archdeacon of Portsmouth, the Venerable H.H. Rodgers, opening the church of the Ascension on 20 May 1936. He was assisted by the parish vicar, Revd C.H. Spinney, the choirmaster, Mr C. Brookes, and the organist, Mr A.J. Green, in the presence of a gathering of 300 parishioners.

The Ascension church was built to serve the rapidly developing congregation at the west end of the village. Fareham Council approved application for the temporary wooden building for three years. It served until it was closed and demolished in 1975. The village chalk pit just shows above the entrance in this 1938 view.

Inside the Ascension church hall. This occasion was a Harvest Supper, with many well-known faces present. The Revd C.H. Spinney is standing at the back and the Wadey family is well represented by Mrs Dorothy Wadey, Mr Dave Wadey and their daughter Joy, third to fifth in, on the second table from the right, in around 1950. Roy Mudd is on the near end of the first table.

Portchester Church Restoration Fund.

Balance Sheet.

Receipts.	£	s.	d.	Expenditure.	£	s.	d.
Donations and Subscriptions	624	9	6	Messrs. Goddard & Sons, Builders	941	15	1
Received in Postage Stamps	31	2	8	Mr. Graham C. Awdry, Architect	96	19	7
Profits from Bazaar and work sold afterwards	229	7	9	Messrs. Sprague & Co., 12,200 circulars and 8,000 envelopes	32	5	0
Box at the Church, 1886, 1887, and 1888	80	13	10	Paid for doing up and directing 10,240 circulars	3	3	0
Bank Interest	32	6	10	Postage of 11,561 circulars	27	10	0
Hampshire Diocesan Society	30	0	0	Rev. A. A. Headley, postages	3	1	7
Offertories at Re-opening Services	29	0	3	Messrs. Sutton & Sons, Printing and Stationery	2	11	0
				1886. Mr. Whiting, Commission on Church box	1	0	0
				1887. Ditto ditto	2	0	0
				1888. Mr. Boyce, ditto	2	5	0
				F. Stewart, collecting stones, & work in Churchyard	1	5	6
				Messrs. Sprague & Co., lithographing "Bills of Quantities"	3	10	6
				Mr. Vennell, Clerk of the Works	46	5	11
				Mr. Wooldridge, Registrar's Fees for Faculty	8	16	4
				Ditto ditto Consecration	2	2	0
				Messrs. Abraham & Sons, curtains, &c.	3	10	6
				Messrs. Hart & Co., brass frames for seats	1	5	8
				Messrs. Beale & Co., cards for same		8	9
				Mr. Darby, brass hooks, &c.		13	9
				Mr. Gilbert, restoring old Bible		9	0
				Messrs. Perkins & Son, heating apparatus	43	15	0
Amount of money still required by the Restoration Committee	170	14	7	Sundry petty expenses	3	2	3
	£1227	15	5		£1227	15	5

The balance sheet of the Church Restoration Fund, 1889. A major renovation of the nave, chancel, tower and belfry was undertaken in the 1880s. In 1888 the old deal square pews were removed. Some twenty oak bench ends were found built into these parts of the church or used as foundations; doubtless these belonged to the church seats before a fire in 1665.

A parade of the Loyal Portchester Lodge of Oddfellows arriving through the lych-gate to St Mary's church, c. 1948. The first four in the main body are, left to right: Percy Pritchard, Nelson Bartlett, Ernest G. Bartlett and Mark Chivers. The young lad on the right is Gordon Bartlett, with his mother and father to his far right. Les Russell has just come through the lych-gate, to the left of the picture.

Three
Schools and Education

Portchester Secondary Modern, now Community, School, was built just prior to 1940 and, if required, could have served during the war as a hospital. Pupils leaving after classes stream out onto White Hart Lane pavements in around 1959.

The only known picture of the old school house, adjacent to Portchester School, c. 1890. The school bell is just discernible on the far gable. Mr Brookes was the last headmaster to live in the house. It was demolished in about 1934 to increase the playground area.

Now the old school is called 'Castle Street Centre' and is a community facility offering a variety of educational courses. In 1892 a wing was added to match the earlier structure to the right.

The gable where the school bell hung for many years, to urge the village children not to be late. Ringing the bell was considered a great privilege for the selected pupil, who not only had to be the best behaved but also the best dressed. Helping on the farm before school was not considered a good excuse for wearing working clothes!

School staff with the headmaster, 1931. Back row, left to right: Mr R.S. Harrison, Miss M. Patterson, Miss M. Wing, Mr Lewer; Front row: Miss L. Sturgess, Mr C.J. Brookes, headmaster, and Miss N.E. Sparks.

The entire staff and pupil body of Portchester School, 1896. The tall girl, fourth in from the left, is Lily May Staples (later Towse) mother of co-author E. John Towse.

A single class of Portchester School, forty-three years later in 1939. The boy in the second row from the back, second from right, is E. John Towse. This picture was taken in almost the same position as the previous one. Ken Tomlinson, May Rivers and Bob Parr are also in the class.

Portchester School bell, manufactured by Warner & Sons, London, in 1874. The bell hung on the gable of the school, which was opened in 1873. It was rung many hundreds of times by Mr Richard 'Gaffer' Bennetts, who was headmaster for over fifty years from the formation of the school. The bell was used to signal school time and play times and was presented to Mr Bennetts on his retirement in about 1918. In 1938 it was erected over the main entrance to the new Ascension church in White Hart Lane but was seldom rung because of the close proximity of the houses. Removed during the war, and lost for many years, it turned up again when the church was demolished.

Pupils at Castle Primary School admiring the old bell and beam in 1971. Back row, left to right: Tracey Buckner, Alan Banting, Janet Taylor, Mark Woodbridge, Sharon Kemp, Teresa Mullens. Front row: Mary Pincott, Roger Underhill, Ronald Hooper, Simon Shawyer, Andrew Burnett, Sonia Banting, Tina Pearce, Dean Pepperell, Karen Taylor, Katherine Ray, Susan Potter, Carol Owtrim.

The so-called Manor House in Castle Street, c. 1920. It was last occupied by Mr Dean Cooper. There is no evidence that this house justified its grand title. It escaped burning down by an incendiary bomb, only to be demolished in about 1950. Empty for a number of years, it was a secret meeting place for some of the boys and girls of the village. It was eventually replaced by Manor House School, which became Castle Primary School.

Grade 2 listed building Reef Cottage, formerly named St Brelades, abuts Castle School. Hampshire-born Stephen Butler Leacock stayed here until his family emigrated to Canada when Stephen was six. He later became a very famous Canadian academic and much revered humorist writer. Stephen's uncle, Revd Charles Butler, who also lived here, was formerly rector of St Mary's church between 1857 and 1869. Stephen Leacock's autobiography refers to his return visit to Portchester in 1921, and to his childhood memories.

A partial view of the original Wicor School, showing the headmistress's office, c. 1963. The school's first headmaster was Frank Hargreaves in 1939. The school finally closed in 1978 and was used as a small farm. Portchester's other windmill, the Wicor Mill, stood nearby on the foreshore until its demolition in 1920.

The new Wicor Primary School, situated in Hatherley Crescent, opened in 1963 to replace the old wooden buildings of the previous school. Pupils from the old school were shared between the new school and the existing Manor House School in Castle Street.

Castle Street Junior School, 1938. Top row, left to right: Kingdom, -?-, James, Hodgeson, Hibbs, Corlett, Marchant, Wadey, -?-. Second Row: -?-,-?-, Eldred, -?-, Scott ?, Blakey, Thomas, Goodeve, Nail, -?-. Third row: -?-, -?-, -?-, Atkin, Cushion, Taylor, -?-, -?-, -?-, -?-. Fourth row: Budden,-?-, Scott, Dawkins, Collett, Fuller, -?-, Saunders, Edwards, O'Sullivan, Hobbs, Maidment, -?-, Exelby, -?-, Clark, Le Pivert, -?-.

Portchester Secondary Modern School, class 1A, 1947. Miss Paice was the teacher. Front row, second from the left is co-author Derek Pearce. In the picture, and still living locally, are Bryan Court, Ray Cooper, Les Cole, Bob Hennessy, Alan Chamberlain and Brian Lemmon. Also in the group are Thelma Carpenter, Mavis Miller and Joan Russell.

This medallion, found near the castle, in the mud, commemorates 100 years of Sunday schools. A hop token found in the same place suggests that it was a mature adult who had lost the two pieces. Hopefully the individual did not lose his life, as some did on the mud, while 'cockling', or digging for bait.

The old Wesleyan Methodist chapel at 49 Castle Street, built in 1867. The only education available to many children from the eighteenth century was through Sunday schools. Until 1933 this chapel was used as a Sunday school for the village children. It then became a riding school and stable, before being converted to a residential house. It is pictured here in 1965.

The village only needed one school in 1911 when this was taken. Headmaster 'Gaffer' Dickie Bennetts, stands proudly with his Portchester School football team. A recently won cup would seem a good reason for this picture. Now Portchester has six schools.

Northern Junior School on the slopes of Portsdown Hill, opened in 1963. Co-author Brian Taylor and his wife Jacky can be seen taking three of their grandchildren, Giles, Josie and Charlie, to school. The curriculum here allows for a detailed interest in local history and classes are well informed on Portchester's past.

Four

Residents and Personalities

Pictured here in the 1950s are Cdr C.E. Hamond, RN DSO, DSC and bar; and William Chester 'Chinta' Pratt, Hampshire Bantam Regiment. Chinta's trilby, always worn, increased his height by three or four inches. In 1914, the Member of Parliament for Birkenhead pressed the War Office for permission to form a battalion of men who were under regulation size but otherwise fit for service. A few days later some 3,000 men, including Chinta, who had previously been rejected as being under height, had volunteered.

Mr and Mrs William and Charlotte Hayter (née Knight) had a family of ten children. This picture of the couple is from around 1910. Their wheelwright business eventually evolved, via carts and carriages, to vehicles and trucks. His sons continued in business and his grandson Robert (Bob) eventually owned a string of garages around the south Hampshire area.

Helen Elizabeth ('Nellie') Hayter's wedding group in the 1900s, after she became Mrs Nellie Knight. This is the back of West End House, West Street, the family home of Mr and Mrs William and Charlotte Hayter, whose large family spread throughout Portchester and beyond.

Mr and Mrs Knott and their son ran the Scout and Guide troops in Portchester. Mr Knott senior was Scout Master for the 1st Portchester Troop, seen here in 1930, and his son followed in his father's footsteps to become Scout Master until some time after 1945.

Mrs Molly Cobham performs the launching ceremony of the newly acquired Sea Rangers rowing boat in around 1961. The boat was named *Mary Rose* and the skipper, seen on the port bow, was Mary Campbell. Cdr and Mrs Cobham were very committed to the Sea Rangers and Scout movements in the district and specifically Portchester.

Four generations of the Durant family, a name going back in Portchester history to at least the eleventh century, seen here in 1930. Left to right: Mrs Durant, her daughter Mrs Wilson, her granddaughter Mrs Knocker, with great-granddaughter Jean Knocker (later Duce).

A family back garden in Castle Street, c. 1918. The men are, from left to right: -?-, Mr Adams, Claude Rootes, Percy Adams, Reg Adams, Harold Wilson. The ladies are -?- , Olive Adams (later Hudson), Edith Adams, Florrie Adams (later Rootes) Mabel Wilson (née Adams), Dulcie Adams (later Smart). The children are -?-, baby Barbara Wilson (later Watson) Reggie Rootes, -?-.

Three generations of the Meatyard family, 1947. Left to right, from the back row down: Mr and Mrs Phillip and Peggy Meatyard; Phil's mother and father, Mr and Mrs Frank and Agnes Meatyard; baby John P. Meatyard, and David G. Meatyard in the drive of their house in East Street from where Phil was running his taxi business.

The house that Phil built, shown here c. 1970. Phil Meatyard assembled this bungalow, just off Castle Street, from a kit, with some help from the rest of the family. Completed in 1965, it remained here until 2002 when it was demolished as part of a large development of nineteen houses called 'Barbican Mews'.

A young Margaret Russell (later Carter) standing at the front gate of one of the homes her family occupied in Portchester, around 1911. The copy of the stone set in the wall is visible in the picture, enlarged alongside the original. Providence Place was built by Henry Leigh in West Street to house some of his tobacco pipe factory workers. This is now the site of the Somerfield supermarket.

Now one of Portchester's oldest native-born residents, Mrs Margaret, or Meg, Victoria Carter, (née Russell) is ninety-six years old. She was born at Pendeen Cottage, opposite Waterside Lane, in 1906. Her father, Henry Russell, was always known as 'Buffer' and her mother, Elizabeth, as 'Bessie'. At sixteen she worked at Worley's teashop in East Street. She married Harold Carter at St Mary's church in 1927.

The display case of Meg's father-in-law, Thomas Carter. A formidable sportsman playing both cricket and football for Portchester, he refused the opportunity to play at national level in the London league because of his market garden business. Mr Carter and his two sons cultivated the fields south of the existing shopping precinct for many years.

Bob Turp, Thomas Carter's grandson, is holding his grandfather's collection of medals and trophies shown above. Inset is his grandfather, wearing the red and white shirt of Portchester Football Club.

This 1930s picture shows, from left to right, George 'Nipper' Dore, Cdr 'Bill' Hamond and Mr Jefferies. Bill Hamond built thirty-four Portchester Ducks, to his own design, in the garden of Myrtle Cottage, Castle Street. The commander had a very distinguished record in the two world wars, being one of the few naval officers to be awarded the DSC in both. He must be credited with starting the first clearance diving in the Royal Navy after he instigated the 'P' parties, which cleared the North French ports of explosives after the Second World War.

Commander Cobham, seen here as a young officer in around 1940, became very active in the Scout movement. He and his wife organized the activities of the Sea Scouts and Sea Rangers for many years. Initially using their home, Noel Cottage in Castle Street, they eventually achieved a purpose-built Scout headquarters for the 3rd Portchester group in White Hart Lane. In 1980 the building was named Cobham Hall in his memory.

Mrs Hilda England (née Hayward) outside daughter Mary Hale's shop, 1980. Mary Hale later restored the old 'Ambrose' shop front back to its original residential frontage, for which she received The Portchester Society Award. The vegetable stall is part of a film set for *Brandon Chase*, which was being produced at the time.

This area around the castle is often used for various film and television productions. *Brandon Chase*, above, included Liza Goddard and Christopher Biggins amongst its cast. Some of the other television series filmed here included *Five Children and It*, *An Unwanted Woman* with George Baker as Inspector Wexford, and recently Adam Hart-Davies's *What the Romans Did for Us*.

The Bartlett family preparing for football practice in around 1941 at Castle End near Peacock Lane, now called Wicor Path. Ernest is in uniform, beside Reg and young Gordon. Behind them is the 'Ambrose' sign for Miss Barr's shop which served 'penny Vantis', a sweet fizzy drink, very popular with the village children.

This 'posse' of 1948 residents set themselves up to rid Castle End of a marauding fox that was eating the chickens, still heavily relied upon for food and eggs during post-war rationing. Left to right: Cdr 'Bill' Hamond, Arthur Towse, 'Jumbo' Hannant, 'Brassy' Ware and Jim Russell. Using a piece of wood, Arthur Towse caught the fox and was awarded the brush.

Five

The Village, Roads and Streets

Castle End, Castle Street, taken from the air by Des Biggs, 2002.

The Cross Roads, Portchester. Note the double-decker bus and Methodist church in the bottom right-hand corner, 1946.

Contemporary view of the Cross Roads by Des Biggs. The Methodist church at the bottom right is one of the few remaining buildings from the old picture. The shopping precinct just south of the bypass has replaced the old main road.

Nelson's Monument, nearly 100ft tall, watches over the Solent and English Channel from the top of Portsdown Hill. Fort Fareham is to the west of the column. Nelson's Monument overlooking Portchester was in position thirty years before the column in Trafalgar Square.

The monument was paid for by voluntary contributions from the British Fleet and erected as a leading mark for the deep channel into Portsmouth Harbour. Ships in Portsmouth Harbour used the mark for 'swinging' their compasses. Mr Gilbert and his horse are working the surrounding farmland in this 1936 view.

Hill Road, previously Abbotts Way, leads to the top of Portsdown Hill. This view shows Portchester's development on the hill slopes. The village chalk pit is now filled with houses.

Early Hill Road before development, around 1926. The three children are all from the Hayter family with Ruby (later Frankum) leading, and her brother Victor and cousin Gladys following. The village chalk pit can again be seen in the background.

Moving down Hill Road into Station Road. These old houses were on the east side, just above the Smithy shown below. Mrs Carter is holding the cat with Mrs Harper by her side, in around 1900.

The north-east corner of the Cross Roads, in around 1930, before the old smithy and the house were demolished for a large Co-operative shop to be built on the site. In 1567 a horse-driven corn mill stood on the site of the old smithy.

The north-west corner of the Cross Roads, c. 1950. The double-decker Southdown bus coming out of Castle Street on its way to Portsmouth was a frequent service at the time.

The north-east corner of the Cross Roads showing the narrow entrance of the tree-lined lane to Cosham. The village policeman lived in the large house on the corner of Castle Street. Just beyond the two small girls are the low walls of the animal compound used for holding any wandering animals until they were claimed by their owners. This was around 1900.

The north-east corner of the Cross Roads opposite the filling station, looking towards Cosham, 1950s.

Harry Worley's Portchester Tea Rooms, here pictured in arond the 1930s. The rooms later became Checkley's in East Street, just beyond the Regent Garage shown in the top picture.

The old A27 in around 1930, running through the centre of what is now the pedestrian shopping precinct towards Fareham. Wheeler's bakery and shop was renowned for lardy cakes and fresh bread. Children from the Castle Street School bought 1d slices of bread warm from the oven after school.

The busy A27 through the centre of Portchester made the creation of a bypass essential. The old Red Lion public house has been replaced by a modern version, almost on the same site but with a less dangerous entrance from the precinct. This view dates from around 1960.

The front of Turret House, here seen on the left, looking back towards the Cross Roads, c. 1910. Turret House's signalling tower was built for the Castle Garrison Commander, who decided that he and his family should be removed from the noise and disruption at the castle, where thousands of prisoners were kept during the Napoleonic Wars.

West Street leads away towards Fareham with the Red Lion showing on the right, in around 1910. The turret on Turret House, now the site of the library and health centre, is just visible. It was used to signal to and from the castle so that the commander could keep in touch with his garrison.

The road west to Fareham, c. 1950. On the left is the entrance to Cornaway Lane as it looked before the roundabout was constructed.

Looking back along West Street towards the Cross Roads, c. 1950. Upper Cornaway Lane, on the left, crosses the main road to Cornaway Lane, which turns to the east into White Hart Lane.

This garden on the north-west corner of the junction faces south in this view from around 1925, which shows Cornaway Lane before the housing development on the west side of the lane. This was where the then headmaster of Castle Street Junior School, Mr Charles Brookes, lived; after him his son Royston lived here, followed by grandson Andrew.

The north-east corner showing the entrance to The Crossways, 1950. The Fairway Roadhouse has long since disappeared, but the site of Huxfords garage is still a modern garage and mini-market.

White Hart Lane looking east, c. 1945. It remained unmade up until the early 1950s, although double-decker buses still managed to move up and down its length.

The modern equivalent of the above, now a busy thoroughfare. Castle Street to White Hart Lane and up Cornaway Lane to the A27 has long been the traditional bus route through the original village.

White Hart Lane from Neville Avenue looking west, c. 1973. This area of Portchester has remained relatively unchanged since the houses were built in the 1930s.

White Hart Lane meets Castle Street at the site of the 1912 Parish Hall in the conservation area. Sadly, the hall and trees were demolished in 2002 allowing a block of six modern flats to be built on the site.

The view from the railway bridge at the station shows the lower end of Station Road, leading towards the roundabout and the entrance to Castle Street. The keep of the castle stands proudly in the background.

The Stores, owned by Webbs, later Meatyard's Store, on the south-west corner of the Cross Roads around 1900. The tree is on the forecourt of the old Railway Hotel.

Meatyard's rebuilt store at the top of Castle Street in around 1930. The stone on the building proclaimed it as 'Devonshire Cott'. It remained on the corner until demolished for the building of Portchester's first bank in 1936.

One of the previous post offices in Castle Street may be seen on the extreme right here in 1930. It remained there for many years before moving to West Street in the 1960s. Castle Street Junior School and Portsdown Hill can be seen to the north.

'Shrub Cottage', seen here in the 1940s and now replaced by 47 Castle Street, was demolished in 1964 for the Doctors Lambert's house and surgery. The terraced house just showing on the right, No. 41, was the old post office at the time of the Boxing Day flood of 1912.

This is one of two terraces which were built for the coastguards. The group of 1930s children contains at least two or three members of the England family, who then occupied No. 86. The small boy between the two girls, Joe, has moved back into the house which had been the home of his family for more than eighty years.

A common occurrence in Castle Street was the twice daily movement of the cows from the meadows and back for milking. On the right is the stepped entrance to the 'so-called' Manor House. The grassed rainwater ditches, running the length of the street here in 1940, were a feature until after 1950.

Further down the street, No. 81, which was called St Brelades in 1921, the time of this photograph, was the home of the Durant family, who can be seen here on a motorbike and sidecar. Mr Arthur Durant drives and Mrs May Durant holds baby Gerald, with daughter Iris riding side-saddle on the pillion. The cow on the left casts a doubtful eye on the mechanical transport.

The thatched cottage on the left, seen here in 1915, was one of a pair destroyed by fire in about 1938. They stood opposite the White Hart public house site. Just beyond, there is the old brewery, then a dairy which became a taxi business and finally a funeral parlour. It is now a terrace of three houses.

The Women's Voluntary Service (WVS) parading past a saluting platform, outside the White Hart public house in 1942. Beer was still being delivered in wooden barrels, as the stack against the car park wall demonstrates.

The old White Hart public house on the north-west corner of White Hart Lane and Castle Street in around 1915. The row of cottages, called 'Box Tree Cottages', filled the space between the 1912 Parish Hall and White Hart Lane before the lane was widened and surfaced.

Modern equivalent of the above, with White Hart Lane on the left. The 'new' White Hart public house was built in about 1938, much further back from the street. A public house has stood on this site for more than 200 years. The large white house on the right is The Retreat, which for many years had a grapevine growing on the south-facing wall.

The 1912 Parish Hall, built of faience blocks, was paid for by the residents of Portchester. The tower on the roof was a wind-blown ventilator. Many village wedding receptions, dances, parties, dinners, exhibitions and shows, including boxing, were held inside. Edgar Taylor, one of a large number of people who tried to save the hall, made this charming drawing.

The commemorative stone in the front corner pillar, which reads: 'This stone was laid by Arthur Lee Esq May 1st 1912 Revd F.J. Sibree MA Vicar'. Arthur Lee was MP for Fareham and the Revd Sibree was the leading figure in obtaining funds and initiating the building of the hall. Initially the building was very much church orientated but rapidly became the centre for village activities. During the Second World War it served many purposes, including Home Guard headquarters and Roman Catholic catechism classes.

The old terraces in Castle Street, Nos 120 to 138, *c.* 1915. A lead veranda protected the front doors of the older terrace, built in the 1840s. West View Terrace was also known as 'The Veranda Terrace'. The veranda was accidentally damaged by a thrown bicycle in the early 1940s and never replaced. It was used, it was said, 'for the war effort'.

The newer of the two terraces was built in around 1911 by Charles Gates and was known by locals and by the postman as 'Merry Terrace'. Postcards, in 1919, arrived successfully with no house numbers needed. The Staples descendants have occupied No. 122 for over ninety years, with four generations living in the house at various times.

Looking back up Castle Street towards the old White Hart on the left and the thatched cottages opposite, in around 1890. Hythe Cottage, on the right, had a hedge which was later replaced by the low flint wall.

Looking down Castle Street from almost the same position as above, c. 1900. The cottage in the centre is the old Quaker Meeting House and immediately next to it, to the south, is the early Wesleyan chapel.

From the bend in the road, the castle keep is almost hidden by the chestnut trees. This would be a visitor's first glimpse of the fortress when walking down Castle Street. The large house, now known as 'Appletrees', is shown prior to rendering with its original façade in around 1950.

This lovely old thatched cottage, for many years owned by the Hurst family, was occupied by Toby Adams and his family until it was destroyed by some young vandals who set fire to the thatch in 1988. It has now been rebuilt and extended. This postcard was sent to France in 1908, was discovered in Paris and recently returned to Audrey Bill in Portchester. It dates from around 1900.

The back of this 1912 postcard reads: 'This is a Photo of the floods we was in that Frank Catmore taken Mrs Adams some Water in a Bucket to her Bed room Window because they cant git down Stairs they ware worse then we ware'[sic].

A modern equivalent of the top picture. The tall old flint house that can be seen in the 1912 view, but was demolished in 1955, was the home of the Mundy family for many years. The father, Mr 'Potter' Mundy, was a general handyman and jobbing builder for the village.

The small opening on the left was once known as 'Mutton Chop Alley' and led to the outbuildings of St Vincent House, which had a Duck punt stowage area. The first house, for many years the home of the Goodall family, has on it a Portchester Society plaque giving the approximate position of the village pillory in 1405. The tastefully-restored beam-fronted cottage won the Fareham Society award for its restoration.

These Duck punts, in 'Mutton Chop Alley', were used prior to 1939 for duck shoots in Portsmouth and Langstone Harbours. A 'blunderbuss' type duck gun was mounted on the foredeck. One popular hunting ground was called 'the Cribs', an area of very small islands to the north of Horsea Island in Paulsgrove Lake. The islands were separated by narrow deep channels at high tide and could easily be navigated by small boats. This picture dates from 1979.

Across the road from 'Mutton Chop Alley' was one of the old vicarages, seen here in around 1940, on the left of the picture. The 1912 flood extended to about here before the rising ground, towards the castle, provided Castle End with a dry area.

At Castle End in the 1930s Long's bakery has its summer canopy up and Ducket House, adjacent, has a thick cover of ivy. The other shop, to the north, with the canopy, is The Bowery Stores. The tall tree at Wisteria Cottage may be seen in both these pictures.

The Memorial Institute, which once served as a school, and the Ivy House stand either side of Portchester's first fire station in around 1915. In here was stored the hand-drawn and hand-operated fire cart. The top of the sliding door has a sign, 'Fire Station'.

The Ivy Rooms in the Ivy House were a very popular tourist attraction, seen here in the 1920s. Here the ivy actually grew inside the rooms and customers had to take their chances while at lunch or tea not to have their meals enhanced by leaves or live specimens from above!

Looking up Castle Street from the 1935 Jubilee Oak; Martell's long greenhouse used to dominate the east side of Castle End in this 1940s view.

Crown House, formerly The Crown public house, was converted to a private dwelling by Admiral H.H. Smith. It had an unobstructed view before the planting of the Jubilee Oak in the grass triangle.

Castle End leads the way to the entrance to the castle through the land gate. The castle keep now towers above the village scene. This scene is of the 1930s.

The way back to Castle End from the land gate, c. 1900. Castle Cottage, on the left, is situated near the site of where the old medieval moat crossed the entrance road. This building was effectively the first 'guard house' on approaching the castle entrance.

Looking north east from the keep in around 1930 towards Paulsgrove shows The Jungle – previously The Old Vicarage, now the Sailing Club – and the old Powder House on the extreme left. Portchester Lake, with the two old wooden wrecks, leads into Paulsgrove Lake. The wrecks in the channel were eventually cleared and the small chalk pit became enlarged as a prominent feature due to extensive quarrying.

The meadows running to the north west before the banks were built up, c. 1920. Portsdown Hill is almost clear of houses. The wooden cottage in Temple Way was extended around a wooden hut, one of three removed from the castle after the First World War. They had been used to house soldiers stationed in the castle.

Six

Pageants, Galas and Outings

A four-in-hand charabanc outside the Railway Hotel on the north-west corner of the Cross Roads, c. 1900. The smartly-dressed passengers are about to depart on a day's outing to Southampton. On the return, late in the evening, apparently, the four horses could not pull the load up Titchfield Hill. The entire party had to disembark and help push.

The 1907 pageant, with a cast of 800, involved most of the village. A number of the cast came from Portsmouth. Here is a line up of local girls – Morris Dancers on the left and Maypole Dancers on the right. The tall girl in the centre is Lily May Staples, and to her right are sisters Flo and Mabel Adams, later to become Lily's bridesmaids.

'Arrival of Queen Elizabeth', Episode V, 1907. The whole pageant was enacted within the inner bailey of the castle. Although the real Elizabeth I is reputed to have visited Portchester, unlike the visits of earlier Kings and Queens, there is no real evidence of her stay.

Another pageant at the castle, 1932. This time most of the cast came from the village. The actor on the row second from bottom, far right, is schoolmaster Mr Charles Brookes. Barbara Curtis, from The Murrels, is in the line-up.

The outer bailey of the castle makes an ideal setting for historical re-enactment societies to recapture a picture of the past. Here, in 1998, Ermine Street Guard first century Imperial Legionaries recreate a formation likely to have been seen around the third century AD within the walls of the original Roman fort.

Near the top of Castle Street the decorated Portchester fire engine is in the procession to the castle to mark the Jubilee of King George V, 1935.

With a background of church and castle walls these four local girls were part of the 1935 Jubilee fancy dress competition. They are, from left to right: Vera Towse, Joan Hill, Audrey Williams and Joyce Sturgess.

This 1946 tableau, thought to be leaving from 'Little Wicor Farm' at the west end of White Hart Lane's junction with Cornaway Lane, is part of a Red Cross display and competition at the castle.

The lorry in front is displaying 'International Friendship' and the one following, also in the top picture, was called 'Health Crossing'. Both won prizes for the best tableau for Red Cross Cadet Unit 3532 in 1946.

This large group of children and parents from the houses on the upper slopes of Portsdown Hill are enjoying VE (Victory in Europe) celebrations. Portobello grove is well represented by Mr and Mrs Len Ancell and their children, Len (junior) and Janet. Also pictured is Roger Trowell, third baby from centre right, held by his mother Mrs Pat Trowell.

The Castle Street VE party, 12 May 1945. Derek Pearce (co-author), first boy on the right, remembers it being a hot day and the chocolate on the cakes melting. The group shown here was almost the entire population of the houses from this part of Castle Street. Mrs Laws organized the party.

Thought to be Queen Elizabeth II's Coronation fancy dress parade held in the castle, 1953. One of the judges below the corner bastion, Mrs Iris Smith, a local schoolteacher, is taking her job very seriously as she studies the line of children.

With their 1953 Coronation hats framing the keep, this pair won the fancy dress prize. They are, from left to right, Michael and David Wells from Neville Avenue.

A long procession of floats and displays in this 1999 gala includes a pipe band, seen here as the parade turned from White Hart Lane into Castle Street.

The Camelot float passes Hythe Cottage as it wends its way to the castle. Charity collectors with buckets accompany the near mile-long procession to collect donations from the pavement spectators.

Gala princesses in the procession on their way to the castle, 1999. Organizer, Alan Simpson and his band of helpers have continued a Portchester tradition of successful summer galas.

A procession from an earlier May Day celebration held in the castle, 1953. The coach and four is heading up Castle Street bearing the newly-crowned Gala Queen Jean Foster and her attendants.

This is 'The Grand Spectacular Finale' of the Portchester Pageant in 1907 in the inner bailey, showing the entire cast, whose numbers almost matched the population of the village at the time.

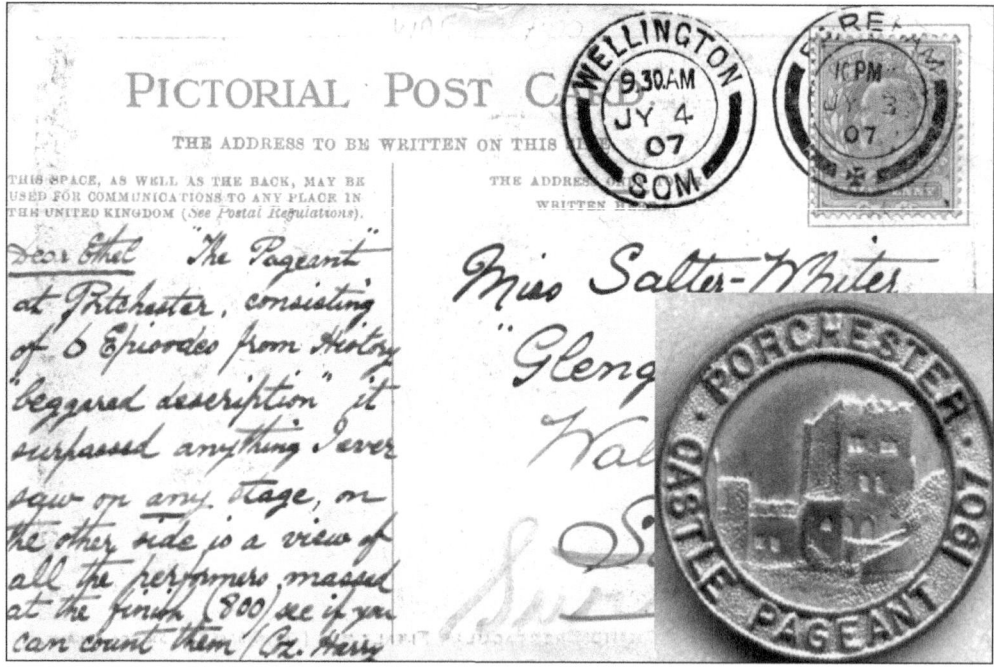

A postcard written by a very enthusiastic audience member in 1907, saying the pageant 'beggered description it surpassed anything I ever saw on any stage' [sic]. The inset shows a rare small cast lapel badge given to some of the leading performers.

Seven
Listed Buildings and Old Houses

The Crown Inn at Castle End, Castle Street, in 1905. The young sailor, Albert Staples, is standing next to the landlord, George Mew. The girl in the pony and trap is thought to be Alice, Albert's sister. Admiral H.H. Smith was resident in 1927 and converted the building to a private residence, Crown House. His commodore's pennant still hangs in St Mary's church.

The surviving limestone stump of Portchester's 'Little Mill', 1950s. Dating from about 1778, the mill was still operating in 1876. Known then as 'Pycroft's Mill', the mill and miller are described in Stephen Butler Leacock's autobiography. The fields along this part of the shoreline could be an archaeological treasure trove, as some areas cover a burial ground and others are known to have been the site of previous buildings.

Portchester House was used as a hospital during the Napoleonic Wars. Many prisoners, mainly French, were held in the castle. Later, the house became the home of the artistic Farmer family. 'Kitty's Breakfast' by Emily Farmer, now in the Victoria & Albert Museum, was painted here, probably using a local girl as a model. Hospital Lane was called Seagate Lane in earlier times. This view dates from around 1920.

The Jungle, Waterside Lane, 1930s. The house was built in late Georgian times as the mess for the officers of the guard at the castle. Later a vicarage, before becoming a private house, it was bought by Portchester Sailing Club in 1968.

The Old Vicarage, a listed building owned by the sailing club and used as their headquarters. Although modernized and extended to include changing rooms and bars, much of the charm of the old house has been preserved.

Thatched Cottage was home to George Dore, master of a sailing barge, and his family from 1913 to 1985. Nearby residents Admiral Smith and Cdrs Hamond and Barnard thwarted two attempts at demolition. Residents shown are, left to right: Jumbo Hannant, Frank Hall, Mrs Corlett, Mr and Mrs Garward, Jim Russell, landlord of The Cormorant for fifty-one years, and Miss Wyatt. This is around 1960.

To the left, Myrtle Cottage, alongside Oriel Cottage. Many of the houses in Castle Street were named after plants. When a Mr and Mrs Miles lived in Oriel Cottage, Ivor Novello was a frequent overnight guest whenever he was playing in a local theatre.

Wisteria Cottage in full bloom, for many years the home of the Russell family. There is a stained-glass window in the Lepers' Squint in St Mary's church, dedicated to Captain Russell RN. The tall tree, shown on page 74, was near the large brick wall on the right.

One of the previous vicarages in Castle Street and once the home of the Revd C.H. Spinney, seen from the back garden, in around 1930. The old scullery and kitchen entrance have long since been demolished along with the stables and outhouses. The large house is now two separate dwellings.

St Vincent House, for many years the home of Admiral Cooke RN. He had a tower built on the house to intercept the semaphore signals between the castle and Turret House. Portchester Society member Sir Michael Moore, right, has just unveiled a commemorative plaque accompanied by residents Cdr Peter Richardson, his wife Joan and Society Treasurer John Towse.

This listed building at 129 Castle Street was used as a Quaker meeting house during the early eighteenth century. This unique cottage has oak beams and flint walls under the later rendering.

Hythe Cottage, 118 Castle Street, is an eighteenth-century listed building. During recent renovations parts of the house were found to be sixteenth century. It has been altered and added to over the centuries, one of a number in the street with a large Inglenook fireplace. The tall chimney, at the back on the right, was thought to be part of an old brewery. This is it in around 1900.

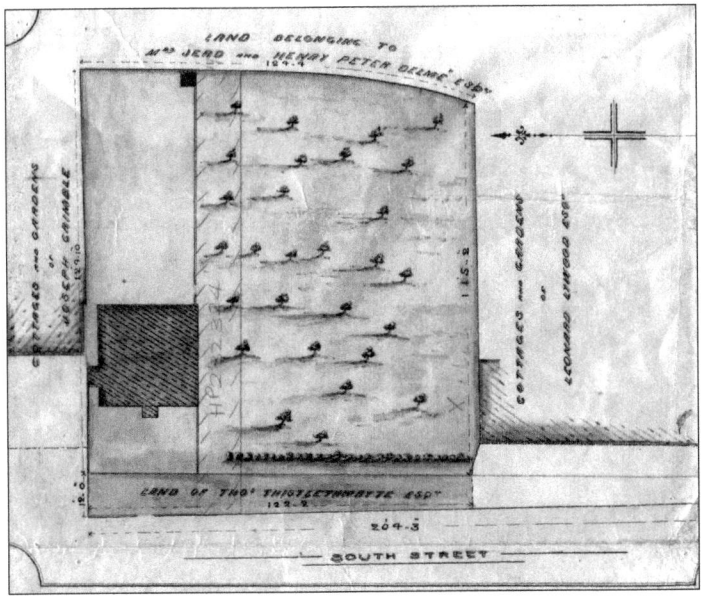

Prior to 1910 the Hythe Cottage garden extended well to the south along what was then South Street. The house was probably self-sufficient, as there was a pigsty in the back as well as a thatched stable for two horses. The wall, originally a hedge, has now doubled in height. This is a copy of the indendature of 1872, when it was sold to Richard Jones for £300.

Alcott House, near the top of Castle Street, had the majority of its windows facing south over the garden. It was a large property and Mrs Alcott, who was an invalid, loved watching and listening to the local children playing and singing. Dame Sybil Thorndyke is said to have played in the garden of Alcott's when she was a child. This photograph dates from the 1950s.

These are the houses that now stand on the Alcott's site. The developer was requested to retain some of the old flint wall from the original house. Careful comparison of the brickwork shows the extent to which the old wall remains.

The demolition of Turret House, with the base of the turret clearly visible at the top right, c. 1960. Originally built for the garrison commander, the house became in turn a school and then a youth club when owned by the church. It is now the site of the library and health centre and has a commemorative Portchester Society millennium plaque.

The rear of Turret House and part of the garden, c. 1940, thought to be the place where the inspiration for Sir John Everett Millais's famous painting 'Bubbles' occurred. Fruit and apple trees in the garden were a source of 'scrumping' for some of the local lads.

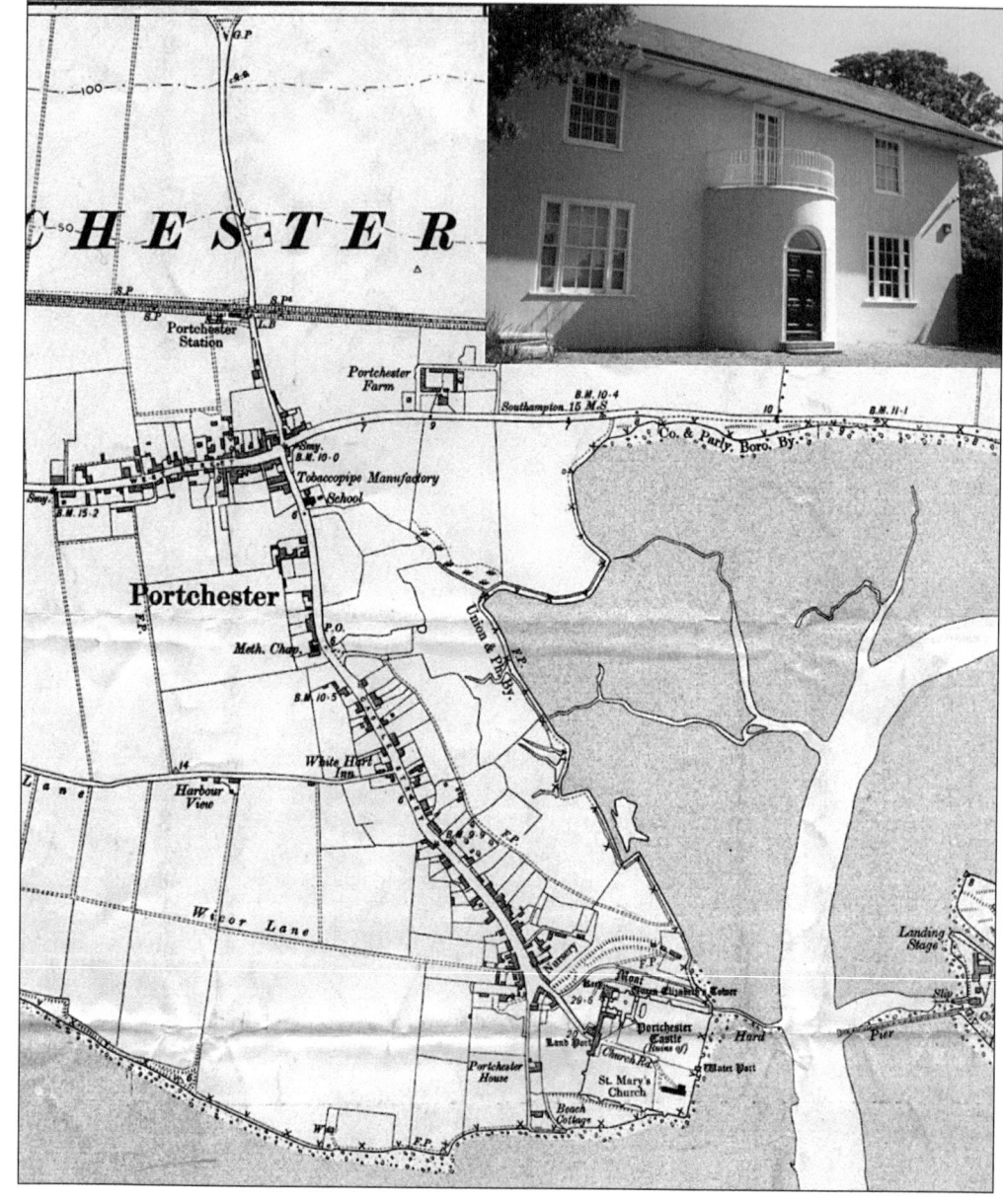

This old map of Portchester, from a survey of 1858, was revised in 1907 and shows a number of distinctive features. The large pier from Horsea Island points towards the old, hard leading from the north-east bastion of the castle. West of Castle Street is almost entirely undeveloped. By the large letter 'S', north of the railway, is the site of Abbots Barn in Hill Road. In 1901 the population of Portchester was 888. On the map, Portchester Farm was 'Murrils', on the north side of East Street. Shown in the inset is the listed eighteenth-century building whose origin, as 'Morals Manor' is uncertain. A document of 1560 shows it as the property of Southwick Priory. Thomas Arthur Curtis farmed here from the late nineteenth century. It was used by Associated British Combustion from 1960 and later developed as a business park in the 1970s.

Eight
Trades and Transport

The Old Bakehouse, at 200 Castle Street, 1876. For many years this was the Long family bakery business. This photograph shows baker George Long and his daughter Helen. The bread cart delivered to houses in Portchester and beyond and Long's lardy cakes were famous all around the area. Passengers on day boat trips from Portsmouth often came to enjoy a lardy cake and bread from Long's, in addition to a visit to the castle.

Houses now obstruct this view of the railway station at Portchester, here pictured in around 1910. Its flint construction and the castellations were clearly influenced by the castle. The line, part of London & South Western Railway, was inaugurated in 1846 and the station opened in 1848.

Porchester was built in 1901 having been designed by R.J. Billinton for the London & Brighton South Coast Railway as a Class E 4, Type 0-6-2 T Tank Engine for mixed-traffic duties. It was handed over to Southern Railways in 1923 and renumbered 31518, becoming part of the Fratton complement of locomotives. It was withdrawn from service in 1955 and presumed scrapped. This photograph was believed to have been taken in Lancing, Sussex, in around 1903.

A party of French sailors about to depart the station following a visit to the castle, where they had been entertained with an open-air meal in the inner bailey in 1905. It is possible that some of their forebears were imprisoned in the castle during the Napoleonic Wars.

Built in 1943 and pictured here in 1945, HMS *Portchester Castle* had a successful war record. Together with other vessels, she was involved in sinking two U-Boats and later became an Air-Sea Rescue vessel. In April 1951 she was in service at Portland Naval Base, until finally being laid up in 1956.

Mr Cooper and his horse in the yard of the old dairy, c. 1920. The old White Hart public house is in the background. Horses were still used by Pearce's Dairy well into the 1940s.

One of the early cars in Portchester, driven by Major Barker, c. 1930. The bungalow in the background is in West Street and still retains a very similar façade.

Hayter & Sons in about 1920, progressing from the earlier wheelwright business, were adding coach-building expertise to the construction of lorries and trucks on a chassis. This fine example has been made for the local firm of market gardeners, C.S. Sturgess & Son, well known throughout Portchester.

Another splendid example of a lorry designed and built by Hayter & Sons for a Portsmouth firm. The 'Fyffes' banana advert on the door, seen here in 1920, is some indication of the considerable length of time that banana boats have been arriving at the port of Portsmouth.

The south-west corner of the Cross Roads, c. 1900. Originally named Devonshire Cott. 1908' [sic] according to a wall stone, it was for many years a shop called 'Webbs' It later became Meatyard's 'The Stores'.

The rebuilding of Webbs stores on behalf of the Meatyards is well underway in this picture, dating from around 1920. The building contractor, F. Hedges, was a local man.

The completed store was run by the Meatyard family until around 1935. A selection of Grafton china souvenirs bearing a Portchester crest was produced for sale to visitors and tourists.

The National Westminster Bank now stands on the site previously occupied by The Stores. Portchester's pedestrian shopping precinct, opened in 1975, replaces part of the old A27 main road.

Hampshire County Council acquired the 120 acre Red Barn Farm, east of Upper Cornaway Lane, in 1909. Farming and market gardening declined and the need for building land increased. In October 1936 some of the land was offered at £650 per acre. The whole area is now housing, with Red Barn County Primary school near the site of the old farm buildings, seen here in 1966.

William Ware Pearce, 1873-1968 and his wife Edith Emily Pring, c. 1905. They farmed Red Barn Farm for many years. When it was sold William started a dairy business. The dairy was located in West Street, on the south side near 'Chalky Walk', where there is now a snooker hall. They had five children. Edith died in 1918, aged twenty-nine.

Portchester Castle from the north shore of Portchester Lake, c. 1910. The vessels shown berthed on the foreshore are close to the present-day site of the large ship building development.

Experimental hovercraft at Vosper's yard, Portchester, 1972. A very large ship construction building now dominates the site, serving an 800-ton ship-lifting facility, believed to be one of the largest in Europe.

Henry James Leigh, 1816-1893, pictured here in around 1880. He was born in the village, the son of James Leigh. Henry established a tobacco clay pipe business on the north side of East Street in 1840. He later moved to another site in Castle Street, just south of the Cross Roads.

The remains of the factory buildings just before demolition, around 1970. The site is now occupied by a three-storey office block. Henry Leigh controlled the business until about 1883 when his nephew, George Meatyard, was made a partner. The business then became Leigh & Co. George ran the business until 1892, when he was succeeded by his sons, Charles and, later, Clifford.

One of the original pipe moulds. At its peak in the 1870s the factory produced 72,000 clay tobacco pipes a week. They were sold throughout southern Hampshire by travelling salesmen using hand and horse-drawn carts which travelled along the coast and returned by way of the South Downs.

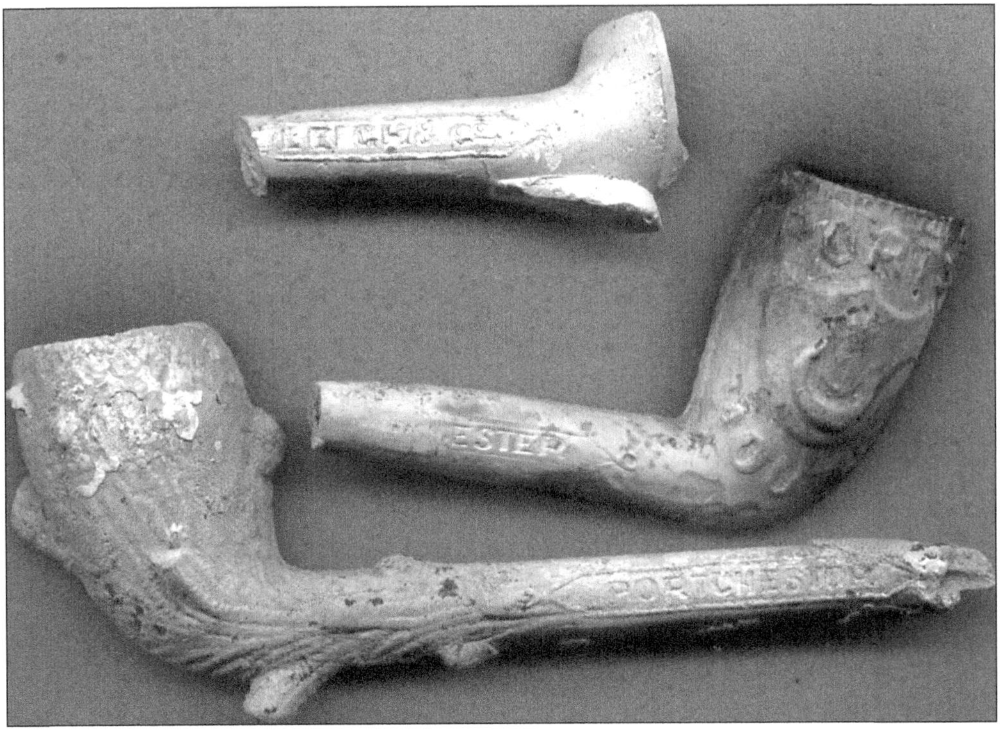

The three fragments shown here were found around the Castle Street area. The middle pipe clearly shows the Portsmouth crest and name. On the reverse of the bowl is the cast of the Town Hall, which later became the Guildhall. Fragments bearing the names Portchester and Leigh & Co on the stems are particularly prized. There are a few collections of complete and nearly complete pipes around the village.

Looking up towards the north end of Castle Street with Noel Cottage on the left in around 1935. On the right is the awning over the shop window of F. Randall's general store, 50 Castle Street. Slightly further up, No. 46 was the post office run by Mrs F. Warren.

The 'mini-market' at 46 Castle Street was opened by Fred Ware when the post office moved to West Street. Mr Pepper, the manager of the shop, is seen leaving. Fred Ware also had a newsagent and stationers at 60 White Hart Lane. This photograph dates from the 1960s.

Geoffrey Rushin's shopfitters business at 39 West Street was run by Geoff's family for thirty-seven years before finally being demolished for housing development in 1999.

On the site of Geoff's business there is now Rushin House, a development by Portsmouth Housing Association in 1999, comprising flats and apartments.

Phil Meatyard's fleet of taxis and his first coach, with son David at the wheel, in the castle car park to the north of the keep in around 1958. An intriguing discussion point by locals and visitors is the long vertical crack seen in the castle keep, which may have been caused by an earth movement in the fourteenth century.

Three cycling visitors to the castle stop for refreshment outside the Crown Inn, now Crown House, at Castle End in the 1900s. In the doorway, the landlord and his wife appear to be using an earthenware flagon of cider to tempt them to quench their thirst.

Portchester firemen proudly compare their self-built new motor-driven fire engine with its pony-drawn predecessor in 1935. Built within the flint walls of the old animal pound, an early fire station in East Street near Newtown, the fire engines are probably decorated for the Jubilee procession.

Volunteer workers, including parents, provide various trade skills to build 'Adurni Hall' adjacent to 'Chalky Walk', a headquarters for the 2nd Portchester Scouts in the 1950s.

One of the Duck punts, probably built by Cdr Hamond, stands, recently completed, outside Myrtle Cottage in around 1930. The Duck punts were used extensively in Langstone and Chichester harbours as well as Portsmouth harbour.

The Portchester Sailing Club transport, for yacht and dinghy crews, heads out to individual vessels in 1946. Walter Sharpe the boatman sits on the bow waiting to bring the club boat back to shore after unloading. The people are, left to right: Peter Wallis, George Dore, Jack Reade, Doug Coyne, Alan Jones and Archie Pay.

Nine
Surrounding Features

The entrance to Station Road from the Cross Roads in an earlier setting, 1930s. The village smithy, on the corner, had existed here as far back as anyone could remember. The blacksmith, Bob Page, bought it in 1913 and stayed there until 1921, when he transferred to a new site in East Street. His son, Arthur, followed him into the blacksmith's trade.

The brewery behind the 'Old Oak' beer house, seen here in around 1940, was located on the south side of West Street. Mr William Goodman was the publican in 1901. It was first mentioned in a trade directory of 1872.

Leading from the Waterside to the walk around the banks protecting the meadows, this right of way brings the pedestrian eventually to the A27, via Hamilton Road. The house shown, called The Jungle, was still a private residence when this photograph was taken in 1945.

Portchester Lake at half tide from the Waterside, showing the old Horsea Pier and the rebuilt steel masts that replaced the 400ft wooden masts of the Royal Naval radio station on Horsea Island. The picture dates from around 1938.

The committee starting boat for the sailing club races is moored alongside the remains of the old Horsea Pier, in around 1947. Admiral Dorling, commodore of the club, is nearest the bow. Cdr Hamond, holding the starting pistol, is second from the left.

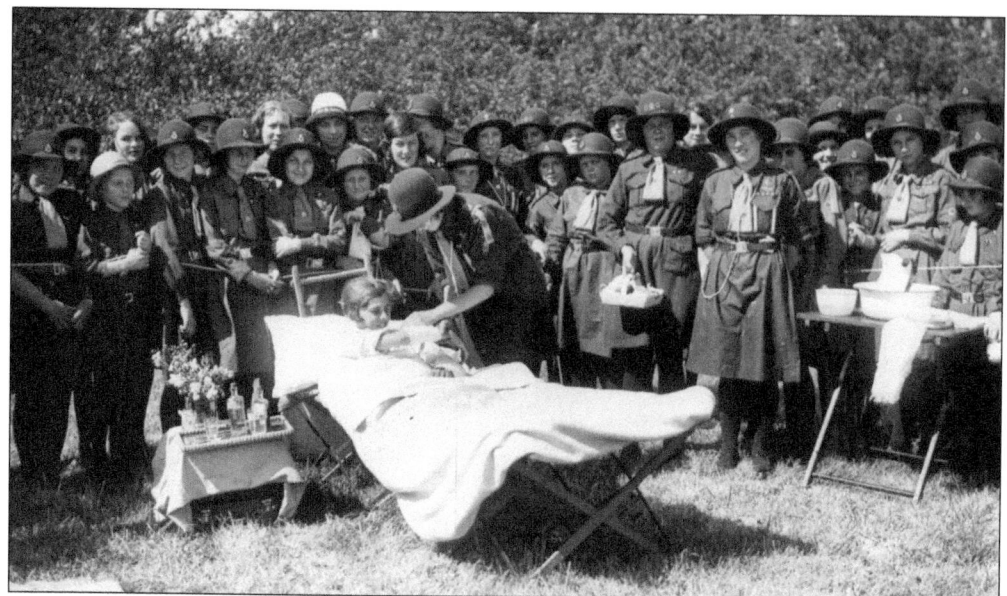

In the garden behind Myrtle Cottage the Portchester Guides practice first aid, around 1933. The 'patient', on the camp bed, is Barbara Wilson (later Watson). Mrs Hamond was Guide Mistress and she continued to refer to 'her girls' even when they were grown-up and married with children!

The outbuilding of Myrtle Cottage in around 1930, where Cdr Hamond built, amongst other boats, thirty-four Portchester Ducks, one of which is shown in the foreground. All thirty-four Ducks were given appropriate duck names, such as *Mallard*. John Maidment, a lifetime member of Portchester Sailing Club, has since built numbers thirty-five, *Shellduck*, and thirty-six, *Merganser II*, to exactly the same design.

Ten
Sport, Sailing and Leisure

Five Portchester Ducks, designed and built by Cdr Hamond, racing at Portchester Lake in 1947. *Shoveller* 10 helmed by John Maidment; *Gadwell* 8; *Blue Wing* 33 helmed by Ray Le Pivert, *Gargany* 16. (The fifth is hidden).

This early team are posing somewhere near the top of Castle Street in around 1900. On the goalkeeper's left is the young Tom Carter, who turned down a professional sports career to manage the family market garden business.

Cup winners and their medals; a successful Portchester Football Team in 1909. From the top, left to right: Bobby Marshall, ? Budd, ? Perry, ? Hayter, ? Durant (goal), Tom Carter, ? Marchant, ? Sturgess, -?-. Second row: ? Adams, ? Ponting, ? Hayter, ? Gates, ? Jeffery, ? Martell. Bottom row: ? Duckett and Toby Francis.

Cricket success, showing the cup in 1910. The site of the picture is unknown. Left to right, standing: ? Marshall, ? Duckett, ? Bone, ? Pelling, ? Sibley, ? Martell, ? Perry. Sitting: ? Hunt, ? Sturgess, Tom Carter, ? Durant, ? Pratt, Jim Russell and ? Marchant. Sir Arthur Conan-Doyle is also said to have played cricket for Portchester during his time in Portsmouth.

Standing, left to right: Bill Wiseman, Gerald Durant (whose father is in the above picture), Ron Harris, Dennis Probee, -?-. Sitting: John Meatyard, Len Ancell (Senior), Wally Walters, Tom Robinson, Bernard Spall, George Wilkinson. England and Portsmouth footballer Jack Froggett, of Castle Street, played cricket for Portchester. In the background a Roman bastion converted to a makeshift pavilion and scoreboard. This is the early 1960s.

Surf Scoter, Duck number 34, in 1946; it was the last Duck constructed by Cdr Hamond in his garden at Myrtle Cottage. It was a privilege for junior members to hold the clenching dolly while the commander riveted the planks inside the hull. The old windlass was, until long after 1945, used for operating the sluice gate to empty and fill the castle moat.

The launching ceremony in what is known as 'The Trollop'. The little girl, Pat Warne, performed the naming ceremony and those present included, Cdr C.E. Hamond, Capt. J.W.S. Dorling, Len Warne, Len Harvey, P. Banister, G. Bosbury, Ray Le Pivert, David Perkins and Ernie Saunders the club boatman. This was 1946.

The Eaglet with Bob Turp at the top, c. 1947. From left to right: Den Bates, Alan Paterson and Des Biggs. Portchester Sailing Club were very generous in their support and encouragement to any of local young people who showed an interest in sailing. The club reformed very quickly following the Second World War, and had a thriving junior section which supplied many boats with young crews. The juniors, when considered competent, took the helm of the Portchester Ducks, which they normally crewed, to compete for the Junior Cup.

Mrs Mary Anne Hamond, wife of the late Cdr Hamond, in 1960, presenting for the first time the Hamond Trophy designed by Peter Scott. They are in the boat compound at the annual Portchester Sailing Club regatta. Almost hidden behind the recipient is club secretary, Les Trelfa.

Portchester Athletic, 1949. Known affectionately as 'the Ath', it brought together village lads from different schools. While there was no connection with Portchester FC, the Ath had its own rare idiosyncrasies. From left to right. back row: Des Biggs, Des Ellis, Mick Gates, Tony Grainger, Harry Jones, and Steve 'Buggy' Goldring. Front row: Den Bates, Brian 'Nibber' Ellis, Alf Piper, Dave 'Mac' McClean and Bob Turp.

A Portchester Boxing Club promotion set up in a field behind the Railway Hotel in Station Road, 1938. On the left is local champion Ronald 'Ginger' Barlett. Prominent boxers of the day were invited to give exhibition bouts. Boxing in Portchester revolved around the enthusiasm of Steve Goldring Snr. Bouts were also organised in the original Parish Hall.

The castle outer bailey was the home ground for both Portchester cricket and football teams until quite recently. The inner moat was an additional hazard for large hits and missed shots at goals. Portchester are seen batting here in 1953, and Geoff Card has just hit the ball.

This old landing was used extensively prior to 1945 for sailors serving at Horsea Island to visit the Portchester hostelries. Mr Saunders, the club boatman, has just arrived, with a junior member helping him. The two torpedo boats on the shoreline just beyond the point were being used as houseboats for two families. This photograph is of around 1948.

Portchester's first purpose-built community centre opened in 1965. It fulfils the needs of the community in a comprehensive and successful manner. The late Miss Betty Balfour-Smith, principal of the Elizabethan School of Dancing, inspired an attractive park recently completed to the north of the centre. The park commemorates her considerable contribution to the society and leisure of Portchester over fifty years.

Some of the back stage crew of the Portchester Players in 1966. Their first production in the new community centre was *A Murder Has Been Arranged*, by Agatha Christie. They are, from left to right: Kay Carter, Nick Carter, Jennifer Beach (prompt), Robert Slater (stage manager), Betty Slater, Angela Alden,-?-, Roger Summers (effects) and Ray Dunster (set design).

Castle meadows have seen many uses over the years. Here is one of the gymkhanas in the early 1960s, with the castle keep providing more than a grandstand view. From medieval times the meadows were salt marshes, later becoming grazing for cattle. During the Second World War they were used to house the evacuated dray horses from Portsmouth that had been forced out of the city by the bombing.

Cricket was played on the meadows formally and informally after 1945. Here in 1955 Warings Ltd play the Yorkshire Nomads, a team that included Norman Yardley, the ex-England and Yorkshire captain. The meadows and banks still provide a recreation area for all to enjoy.

This rare picture shows a birthday picnic in the village chalk pit on Portsdown Hill, c. 1920. These were the family and friends of schoolmaster Mr Charles Brookes. His son Royston sitting on the right with rather a lot of hair is groomed and dressed in similar fashion to the boy in the famous portrait of 'Bubbles' by Millais.

This is the north-east bastion of the castle before the sea wall promenade was constructed, here pictured in around 1938. Kathleen Drake is on the right of the picture with her two cousins. She eventually married the boy in the top picture, Royston Brookes. They lived at The Bungalow in Portchester Road, the north-east corner of the junction with Cornaway Lane.